GW01087089

NOTES TO

THIS publication is divided into five parts: Descriptive, Handling, Operating Data, Emergencies, and Illustrations. Part I gives only a brief description of the controls with which the pilot should be acquainted.

These Notes are complementary to A.P.2095 Pilot's Notes General and assume a thorough knowledge of its contents. All pilots should be in possession of a copy of A.P.2095 (*see* A.M.O. A93/43).

Words in capital letters indicate the actual markings on the controls concerned.

Additional copies may be obtained from A.P.F.S., Fulham Road, S.W.3, by application on R.A.F. Form 294A, in duplicate, quoting the number of this publication in full— A.P 1578C, K, L, M, N & P—P.N.

Comments and suggestions should be forwarded through the usual channels to the Air Ministry (D.T.F.).

AIR MINISTRY   AIR PUBLICATION 1578C, K, L, M, N & P—P.N.
January 1944   *Pilot's Notes*
(*Reprinted May* 1944)

WELLINGTON III, X, XI, XII, XIII AND XIV—PILOT'S NOTES

2nd Edition.   *This edition supersedes all previous issues.*

LIST OF CONTENTS

PART I—DESCRIPTIVE

3

ENGINE CONTROLS *Para.*

OTHER CONTROLS

PART II—HANDLING INSTRUCTIONS

PART III—OPERATING DATA

PART IV—EMERGENCIES

PART V—ILLUSTRATIONS

PART I

DESCRIPTIVE

NOTE.—The numbers quoted in brackets after items in
the text refer to the key numbers of the illustrations in Part V.

INTRODUCTION

A.L.2
Part I
Para. 1

1. The Wellingtons III and X are equipped as medium bombe
(some are used for training purposes), and the Wellingtons X
XII, XIII and XIV for general reconnaissance duties wi
Coastal Command.

The Mks. XI and XIII carry torpedoes, alternatively dept
charges, and operate by day; the Mks. XII and XIV are each fitt
with a Leigh light in the mid-under turret and carry dept
charges only.

The Mks. XVII and XVIII are Mk. XI and Mk. XIII aircra
respectively, converted for special training purposes wi
A.D.G.B.

The corresponding Marks of Hercules engine are as follows:

Mark III	..	..	Hercules XI
Mark X ..	..	..	Hercules VI or XVI
Mark XI ..	..	..	Hercules VI or XVI
Mark XII	..	..	Hercules VI or XVI
Mark XIII	..	..	Hercules XVII
Mark XIV	..	..	Hercules XVII
Mark XVII	..	..	Hercules VI or XVI
Mark XVIII	..	..	Hercules XVII

Each is fitted with Rotol electric or de Havilland hydromatic ful
feathering propellers. Some Mk. III aircraft have Rotol hydraul
propellers.

- -

FUEL AND OIL SYSTEMS *(see* Fig. 4)

2. **Fuel tanks**

(i) *Normal tanks.*—Two main tanks in each wing supply the
feed pipe through non-return valves, and a tank in each
nacelle supplies the same pipe through a cock controlled
from the fuselage. These three tanks on each side supply
the engine-driven pumps through main tank cocks (Cp

and Cs), and the pumps supply the engines through corresponding master cocks (Ep and Es). The capacities of these tanks are as follows:

2 Front wing tanks .. 150 gallons each

2 Rear wing tanks .. 167 gallons each

2 Nacelle tanks.. .. 58 gallons each

(ii) *Auxiliary tanks:*

(*a*) *Mk. III and X aircraft.*—In addition to the normal tanks, an auxiliary self-sealing tank of 140 gallons capacity can be installed in each outer bomb cell. These tanks supply the main feed line for each engine through corresponding non-return valves and on-off cocks (Dp and Ds). Certain aircraft fitted with a high-capacity bomb beam carry an auxiliary tank of 295 gallons capacity in the bomb compartment and this is connected to the auxiliary tank cock (Ds.). Tropicalised Mk. X aircraft carry two 55-gallon tanks when on reinforcing flights.

(*b*) *Mk. XI, XII, XIII and XIV aircraft.*—Up to three auxiliary tanks can be carried, one in each bomb cell. Fuel in these tanks flows through corresponding non-return valves and on-off cocks (Dc, Dp and Ds) into the suction balance pipe and so to the main feed lines. The following alternative tankages can be carried:

(i) One 185-gallon tank in the centre bomb cell.

(ii) Two 140-gallon tanks, one in each outer bomb cell.

(iii) One 185-gallon tank in the centre bomb cell and one 140-gallon tank in the starboard bomb cell (when only one torpedo is carried).

(iv) Three 185-gallon tanks, one in each bomb cell (for reinforcing flights).

The centre bomb cell tank is divided into two partially isolated cells. The three-way selector cock (Dc) allows fuel to be drawn from only one cell at a time, but on some aircraft the two cells are connected separately to the two cocks Dp and Ds and can, therefore, be used simultaneously.

7

3. **Balance cocks.**—The fuel systems for the port and star-board engines are connected by a pressure balance cock (A) (63) and a suction balance cock (B). These cocks are normally kept shut, but the pressure balance cock (A) may be opened if failure of either engine pump is suspected, and the suction balance cock (B) may be opened to enable either engine pump to be fed by tanks on the opposite side.

4. **Tank cocks.**—The pilot can shut off the fuel supply to an engine by closing the corresponding engine master cock (Ep or Es) (61). The pressure balance cock (A) is also under his control. The remainder of the cocks, however, are under the control of the crew and are as follows:

(i) The main tank cocks (Cp and Cs), remotely controlled by handles at the port and starboard sides of the fuselage, immediately forward of the spar centre section.

(ii) The nacelle tank cocks controlled by cables beside the main tank cock handles.

(iii) The suction balance cock (B) and the auxiliary tank cocks (Dc, Dp and Ds) immediately aft of the spar.

> NOTE.—Cocks Cp, Cs and B are three-position cocks, but may be regarded as ON-OFF cocks, as two positions only are used. Cock Dp on Mark X aircraft fitted with two 55-gallon tanks in the port bomb cell is a three-position cock.

5. **Fuel handpump.**—There is a fuel handpump aft of the spar for priming the fuel system (if necessary) and supple-menting the supply of either engine-driven pump. The handpump is connected between the suction and pressure balance pipes on the port side of the pressure balance cock (A); this cock must be open to feed the starboard engine from the handpump, and the suction balance cock (B) must be open for the handpump to draw from the star-board tanks. An ON-OFF cock (H) controls the supply from the suction balance pipe to the handpump.

6. **Fuel gauges.**—Contents gauges for all tanks except the nacelle and centre bomb cell tanks are fitted. To obtain readings operate the pushbutton (9) on the pilot's instru-ment panel or the pushbutton near the gauges on the electrical panel.

7. **Fuel pressure warning lights.**—Two fuel pressure warning lights (22), one for each engine, are fitted on the right-hand side of the pilot's instrument panel and come on when the pressure drops below $1\frac{1}{4}$ lb./sq.in. They are not fitted on Mk. III aircraft.

8. **Oil tanks.**—Each engine has one oil tank, holding 16 gallons, mounted on the front of the nacelle fuel tank. An auxiliary oil tank in the fuselage, aft of the spar, for use on long-range flights, holds 15 gallons and incorporates a handpump to enable oil from the auxiliary tank to be transferred to either of the nacelle tanks through a two-way selector cock in the delivery pipe nearby. (For management of auxiliary tank and pump *see* para. 38.) The oil dilution valves are operated by two pushbuttons, one for each engine, on the electrical panel aft of the cockpit.

9. **Oil tank low-level indicators.**—Two red warning lights (16), one for each main oil tank, are fitted on the pilot's instrument panel and a duplicate pair on the rear side of the wing spar. These light up when the oil reaches a dangerously low level and give warning that the hand-pump must be used to replenish the main tanks.

MAIN SERVICES

10. **Hydraulic system**

(i) *Mk. III and X aircraft.*—Two engine-driven hydraulic pumps are mounted on the port engine; one pump operates the two gun turrets and the other pump supplies the following general services:

> Undercarriage
> Flaps
> Bomb doors
> Carburettor air-intake shutters
> Windscreen wipers.

(ii) *Mk. XI, XII, XIII and XIV aircraft.*—There are three pumps driven by the port engine, one pump supplies the services listed above, a second operates the rear gun turret, and the third pump operates the front gun turret on Mk. XI and XII aircraft and the mid-under turret on Mk. XII and XIV aircraft.

(iii) *All Marks.*—A handpump (81) to the right of the pilot's seat will operate any of the general services through the normal lines if the engine-driven pump has failed, or if the port engine is stopped. If the normal hydraulic system fails to operate these services by either the engine-driven pump or the handpump, the undercarriage may be lowered by an emergency hydraulic system (*see* para. 66)

11. **Pneumatic system.**—Two compressors are driven by the starboard engine; one operates the automatic controls and the other supplies pressure for the wheel brakes and the fuel jettison valves. A suction pump is driven by each engine, one pump operating the blind flying instrument panel and the other acting as a reserve. A pump change-over cock control (84) is fitted to the right of the seat and there is a gauge (25) to the right of the centre instrument panel.

12. **Electrical system**

(i) *Mk. III aircraft.*—A 1,500 watt generator on the starboard engine supplies 24 volts D.C. for the following services:

> All lighting
> Engine starting
> Propeller feathering and pitch changing (Rotol electric type)
> Pressure-head heating
> Fuel contents gauges
> Undercarriage and flap indicators
> Radio and beam approach
> Fire-extinguisher system
> Camera heating
> Oil dilution valves
> Operation of flotation gear
> Release and inflation of dinghy

(ii) *Mk. X aircraft.*—Two 1,500 watt generators, one on each engine, supply 24 volts D.C. for the above general services.

(iii) *Mk. XI and XIII aircraft.*—One 1,000 watt generator on each engine supplies 24 volts D.C. for the above general services and A.C. for the special radio equipment.

(iv) *Mk. XII and XIV aircraft.*—Two 1,500 watt generators, one on each engine, supply 24 volts D.C. for the above general services. In addition, the port engine generator supplies A.C. for the special radio equipment.

D.C. for the Leigh light is supplied by a separate generator on the starboard engine.

(v) *All Marks.*—The external battery socket for ground starting of the engines is under a hinged panel, on the starboard side of the fuselage, below the main plane leading edge. The ground/flight switch is on the starboard side of the fuselage, just forward of the main spar.

AIRCRAFT CONTROLS

13. **Flying controls.**—These are of the conventional type. The rudder bar is adjustable for reach by means of a star-wheel (35) at the rear of its mounting. This can be rotated in flight by the feet, clockwise rotation shortening the reach. Dual controls, coupled to the main controls, can be mounted on a special floor extension forward of the starboard seat.

14. **Trimming tabs.**—The elevator and rudder trimming tabs are operated by a single control (59) which works in the natural sense. There is a fine adjustment control (60) for the elevator tabs to the left of this control. The aileron trimming tab (port only) control is a rotatable handle (65) with a lock-release grip, immediately outboard of the elevator and rudder trimming tab control, and works in the opposite way to the natural, i.e. turning clockwise raises the starboard wing.

15. **Interconnection of elevator trimming tabs and flaps.**—When the flaps are fully lowered they cause the aircraft to become " tail-heavy "; the flaps are, therefore, interconnected with the elevator tabs so that lowering of the flaps automatically raises the elevator tabs and counteracts the " tail-heaviness ".

It is essential that the elevator trimming tab control *should not be forward of* the central position before the flaps are lowered, or damage to the tab control mechanism may result. On most aircraft a spring catch is fitted which allows the pilot to feel the central position on moving the control.

16. **Undercarriage control.**—Raising and lowering of the undercarriage and tailwheel is controlled by a lever (31) in the centre of the instrument panel which has automatic safety catches locking it in the UP or DOWN positions. These catches must be freed by the catch release before the lever can be operated. Each main wheel unit is provided with mechanical up and down locks which automatically lock the unit in the UP or DOWN position as soon as it is fully retracted or lowered. The locks are automatically released by hydraulic power immediately the undercarriage selector lever is moved to the UP or DOWN position. Correct operation of the locks is indicated by the normal undercarriage indicator, with the electrical circuit of which they are interconnected.

17. **Undercarriage indicator.**—On Mk. III aircraft the indicator (11) shows as follows:

All units locked DOWN	..	Three green lights
All units unlocked ..	..	No lights
All units locked UP..	..	Three red lights

but on the later Marks the indicator shows as follows:

All units locked DOWN	..	Three green lights
All units unlocked ..	..	Three red lights
All units locked UP	..	No lights

The indicator switch (49) is interlocked so that it must be on when the ignition switches are on. The indicator DOWN lights are duplicated (on Mk. III aircraft the red lights are also duplicated, but not the tailwheel light), and in the event of failure of a lamp the duplicate set can be brought into circuit by pulling out (or pushing in) a knob in the centre of the dial case. In addition, counterclockwise rotation of this knob operates a dimmer screen.

18. **Undercarriage warning horn and light.**—An electric horn behind the pilot's seat sounds and a red light beside the undercarriage indicator lights up if both throttles are closed and the undercarriage is not locked down. The horn can be tested by pressing the test pushbutton (8) with the indicator switch closed. The light goes out when the horn stops. The light is not fitted on Mk. III aircraft.

19. **Flap control.**—The flap control lever (29) is retained in its neutral position by a spring-loaded catch which is released for operation by depressing the knob. The flaps are interconnected with the elevator tab control (*see* para. 15). The flap indicator (36) is switched on by the undercarriage indicator switch.

20. **Wheel brakes.**—Twin operating levers (40) for the pneumatic wheel brakes are provided on the control column handwheel; they are compressed either singly or simultaneously to apply both brakes. The brakes can be applied in the fully locked position for parking by engaging the locking slide (41). The system provides for differential braking by virtue of rudder bar movement when taxying. A triple pressure gauge (18), showing the main supply pressure and the pressure at each brake, is fitted on the right of the instrument panel.

21. **Flying control locking gear.**—The flying controls can be locked in their neutral position by means of a triangular spring-loaded frame, hinged beneath the window ledge on the port side of the cockpit, and a detachable hinged nuisance bar. When not in use, the former is secured by a strap and pin to the side of the cockpit, and the latter is stowed on the starboard side of the cabin gangway.

ENGINE CONTROLS

22. **Throttle and mixture controls.**—The two throttle levers (46) are interconnected with the corresponding mixture control levers (53) so that if the throttle is moved out of the weak mixture cruising range, the mixture lever will, if in the WEAK position, return to the rich (NORMAL) position. On Hercules XVI and XVII installations there are no pilot's mixture control levers, control being fully automatic. An economical mixture strength is obtained by keeping at or below +2 lb./sq.in. boost. Pending the introduction of a warning light to indicate the economical cruising boost position of the throttle levers, a white line is painted on the quadrant and the levers. On certain modified engines a position midway between the climbing and economical cruising boost settings gives better

economy on the climb after the boost has fallen to +4 lb./sq.in., and this position will be indicated by a second white line. A friction lever (47) is provided for clamping the throttles in any position to prevent movement due to vibration.

23. Propeller controls

(i) The speed control levers (56), common to all three types of propeller, are at the rear of the engine control quadrant and are moved forward to increase r.p.m. The feathering pushbuttons (6 and 15) for the hydraulic types are on the instrument panel.

(ii) The controls for the electric propellers (if fitted) are on the instrument panel and are as follows:

(*a*) *Safety switches.*—These should always be ON in flight as they control the supply to the propeller pitch mechanism and feathering circuits. If an excessive load is applied during any operation, the safety switch is automatically thrown to OFF. If this happens the switch should be reset to ON at the end of about half-a-minute.

(*b*) *Selector switches.*—Each switch can be moved to three different positions other than the central one, in which the propeller operates in fixed pitch. The two lower positions are for manual INCrease and DECrease of the r.p.m. respectively, and when the switch is moved to either of these positions it must be held there until the desired r.p.m. are attained; on being released it will return to the central position. In the upper (AUTO) position, the propeller operates under constant speed control.

A.L.2
Part I
Para. 23
(ii) (*c*)

(*c*) *Feathering switches.*—Are moved upward for rapid feathering and function whatever the position of selector switches. Feathering can be effected slowly, using substantially less current, by holding corresponding selector switch down in DECrease r.p.m. position. In either case, when propeller is fully feathered selector switch should be set central. On later aircraft having Rotol electric propellers, selector and feathering switches are combined in a single switch which operates as follows:

For manual control DECrease r.p.m. is obtained by moving lever to left and INCrease r.p.m. by moving it to right. Lever returns to central on release. AUTOmatic control is obtained with lever in upward position. To feather propeller, knob of lever must be pulled outwards and then moved downwards.

24. **Supercharger control**—The control (54) aft of the throttle levers may be locked in either the MEDIUM (M ratio) or FULL (S ratio) positions by a spring catch which is released by depressing the lever. On Mk. XI, XII, XIII and XIV aircraft the control is locked in M ratio.

25. **Carburettor air intake control.**—The lever (55) at the side of the supercharger control may be locked in either the COLD or WARM positions by a spring-catch which is disengaged by depressing the lever. The shutters are hydraulically operated.

26. **Cowling gill controls.**—The gills are opened and closed by handles (37) which are turned clockwise to open.

27. **Oil cooler shutters (Mk. III aircraft only).**—The oil cooler shutters are operated by " Exactor " hydraulic controls to the right of the pilot's seat.

28. **Slow-running cut-outs.**—The controls (57), which are spring-loaded handles, are aft of the engine control box and each must be pulled and held out to stop the corresponding engine after the throttle is closed and before switching off the ignition.

29. **Priming pumps.**—An induction system priming pump, for use when starting, is mounted in each engine nacelle. A three-way priming cock inside each undercarriage wheel housing allows for priming with high volatility fuel from an outside source.

30. **Engine-starter and booster-coil pushbuttons.**—These (5 and 17) are on the centre instrument panel.

31. **Boost gauge reversal control.**—If one of the boost gauges fails, the boost gauge of the other engine can be used in its stead by pulling out the boost gauge reversal control (28).

OTHER CONTROLS

32. **Bomb doors.**—The bomb doors are operated by a handle (43) which can be moved to the OPEN or CLOSED position, after releasing the lock, by depressing the spring-loaded thumb-knob. The handle is coupled with the bomb release master switch (45) so as to prevent the release of bombs until the control is in the OPEN position.

33. **Bomb/depth-charge release control.**—The pilot can release the bombs or depth-charges by means of the pushbutton (42), provided that they have been selected by the bomb aimer and the master switch is on. (For jettisoning of bombs and depth-charges *see* para. 67.)

34. **Torpedo release controls (Mk. XI and XIII aircraft only).** Two pushbuttons (39), for port and starboard torpedoes, are provided on the control column handgrip. Each is covered by a safety shield.

35. **Heating controls.**—Exhaust-heated air is supplied from both engines via ducts, from which branch pipes supply the various crew stations. The main supply is controlled by a push-pull rod at the wing spar extensions on each side of the fuselage. The pilot's supply is controlled locally by a knob (83) on the diffuser (58) below and slightly forward of his seat.

36. **Landing lamps.**—Two retractable landing lamps in the port wing are raised and lowered by an " Exactor " hydraulic control lever (66) which can be locked in any desired position by a spring-loaded catch which is released at the top of the lever. Either lamp can be lighted, the other acting as a reserve, by operating the three-position switch (44) on the port side of the cockpit.

37. **Reconnaissance flares.**—From three to eleven flares are stowed vertically in racks on the starboard side, immediately aft of the cabin, and the launching tube is mounted amidships on the starboard side of the fuselage. An alternative arrangement of three or six loaded flare chutes in the mid-turret position is fitted in certain aircraft and a flare launching switch panel is fitted in the bomb-aimer's compartment.

PART II

HANDLING INSTRUCTIONS

All handling speeds are quoted for aircraft with the static side of the A.S.I. connected to the pressure head. The equivalent speeds in knots are quoted in brackets. The corresponding speeds for aircraft with the A.S.I. connected to the static vent in the side of the fuselage are given in para. 61.

38. Management of fuel and auxiliary oil systems

(i) *Use of balance cocks :*

(*a*) The pressure balance cock (A) should be turned ON only when an engine fails due to lack of fuel. It should be kept ON only if the engine cannot be supplied otherwise (i.e. if its pump has failed).

(*b*) The suction balance cock (B) should always be OFF unless it is necessary to feed either engine from tanks on the opposite side or, in certain cases, when auxiliary tanks are used.

(ii) *Normal fuel system*

The following recommended procedure ensures the fullest possible use of fuel, and should be studied in conjunction with the Fuel System Diagram (Fig. 4) in Part V.

(*a*) The nacelle tanks should always be filled, even it it is unnecessary to carry full fuel capacity, and their contents held as a reserve until all main tanks are exhausted.

(*b*) The operation of the nacelle tank cocks should be checked after take-off to ensure that the wire controls function correctly in flight. The pre-flight check may have been satisfactory, but the flexing of the wings in flight may interfere with the movement of the wire controls.

(*c*) Take off and fly on the main tanks, with both balance cocks closed and the nacelle tank cocks OFF.

(*d*) When an engine commences to cut through lack of fuel (this will be indicated by the appropriate fuel pressure warning light) open the pressure balance cock (A). This will revive the engine immediately and there is, therefore, no danger in allowing an engine to splutter through lack of fuel, except when coming in to land.

(*e*) Pull ON both nacelle tanks.

(*f*) Turn OFF the pressure balance cock (A).

A.L.4
Part II
Para. 38
(ii)
(*g*) (*h*)
(*i*)

(*g*) Nacelle tank cocks should not be turned ON until one engine fails due to lack of fuel. This will ensure that the Captain will have a *known* amount of fuel when the main tank supply is exhausted.

(*h*) Nacelle tank cocks should, however, always be pulled ON before landing, if the sufficiency of fuel remaining in the wing tanks is in doubt.

(*i*) During an approach and landing both engines should not be run on the tanks in one wing only, as there is a possibility of fuel starvation on opening up to take-off power.

A.L.2
Part II
Para. 38
(iii) (*a*)

(iii) *When auxiliary fuel tanks are fitted.*

(*a*) Fuel in the auxiliary tanks should be used early in flight, but the change-over should not be made below 3,000 feet.

(*b*) The order of use of the tanks should be so arranged that both engines do not run short of fuel simultaneously (*see below*). In all cases, when one engine fades for lack of fuel (this will be indicated by the appropriate fuel pressure warning light), open the pressure balance cock (A) which will revive it immediately. This cock should be closed again as soon as the fresh supply has been turned ON.

(*c*) *Recommended order of use of auxiliary tanks:*

(1) *When an equal amount of fuel is available on each side of the suction balance cock:* (Two tanks of equal capacity in the outer bomb cells, or a 185-gallon tank in the centre bomb cell connected to cocks Dp and Ds.):

Both balance cocks must be kept OFF.

Shortly before the auxiliary tanks are due to run out, change over to the main tanks on one side and empty the auxiliary tank on the opposite side. Repeat this procedure for the second auxiliary tank. Turn OFF the auxiliary tank(s) when empty.

(2) *When a greater amount of auxiliary tank fuel is available on the port side of the suction balance cock:*

(A 185-gallon tank in the centre bomb cell connected to cock Dc, and other auxiliary tanks) :

Both balance cocks must be kept OFF.

If a 140-gallon tank is carried in the starboard bomb cell, empty the rear half of the 185-gallon tank first, and then change over to the front half; this will be done before the 140-gallon tank is empty. When the starboard auxiliary tank is empty, open the suction balance cock (B) and run both engines on the remaining auxiliary fuel. Shortly before the fuel is due to run out, turn ON the starboard main tanks, close the suction balance cock (B) and exhaust the auxiliary tanks on the port engine. Then change over to the port main tanks and turn OFF the auxiliary tanks.

NOTE.—This will mean that the starboard main tanks will empty first. When they do, both nacelle tanks remain as a known reserve, plus a small extra quantity in the port main tanks which in the last resort can be used for both engines by opening the suction balance cock (B).

(3) *When a greater amount of auxiliary tank fuel is available on the starboard side of the suction balance cock:*

(A 140-gallon tank in the starboard bomb cell and two 55-gallon tanks in the port bomb cell):

Both balance cocks must be kept OFF.

When the port auxiliary tanks are empty, open the suction balance cock (B) and run both engines on the remaining fuel. The procedure detailed in (2) above then applies, but in the reverse sense.

(4) *When a 185-gallon tank in the centre bomb cell is connected to cock Dc, or a 295-gallon tank is connected to cock Ds, and no other auxiliary tanks are carried:*

As (2) and (3) above, except that the suction balance cock (B) must be ON from the time of first changing over to the auxiliary tank. Shortly before the auxiliary tank is due to run out, the main tanks on the opposite side should be turned ON, the suction balance cock (B) turned OFF and the auxiliary tank exhausted on one engine. The final residual fuel will then be in the port or starboard main tanks according to the bomb cell in which the auxiliary tank is carried.

(iv) *Emergency operation of wing fuel tanks:*

In the event of a wing tank being damaged, the following sequence of operations should be carried out :

(*a*) Turn ON the suction balance cock (B).

(*b*) If fuel remains in the damaged tank, turn OFF the main tank cock (C) on the good side so as to use up any remaining fuel in the damaged tank.

(*c*) When the engines cut* :

Turn OFF the main tank cock (C) on the damaged side.
Turn ON the main tank cock (C) on the good side.

(*d*) When the engines cut again* :

Pull ON both nacelle tank cocks.
Turn ON the main tank cock (C) on the damaged side.
Turn OFF the suction balance cock (B).

* Or earlier if considered advisable.

A.L.6
Part II
Para.
38 (v).

(v) *Operation of the auxiliary oil tank :*
On long range flights necessitating the use of auxiliary fuel tanks, the auxiliary oil tank should be operated as follows : One gallon of oil should be transferred to each main oil tank after four hours of flight and thereafter every two hours. One gallon of oil is transferred by selecting the desired main tank and giving 24 complete (back and forward) strokes of the handpump.

39. **Preliminaries**

(i) Check fuel cock settings in fuselage :

Main tank cocks (Cp and Cs)	On
Nacelle tank cocks	Off
Auxiliary tank cocks (Dp, Dc and Ds) ..	Off
Suction balance cock (B)	Off

(ii) If Rotol electric propellers are fitted check :

Master switches ..	..	ON
Feathering switches	..	NORMAL
Selector switches ..	..	AUTO

(iii) Check that undercarriage selector lever is locked DOWN.

(iv) Switch on undercarriage and flap indicators and test undercarriage warning horn and light (if fitted).

40. **Starting engines and warming up**

(i) Set pilot's engine master cocks (Ep and Es) ON and the pressure balance cock (A) OFF.

(ii) Set engine controls as follows :

Throttles	..	$\frac{1}{4}$ inch open
Mixture controls (if fitted)	..	NORMAL
Propeller speed controls ..	..	HIGH R.P.M.
Supercharger control ..	..	MEDIUM
Carburettor air-intake control	..	COLD
Cowling gills	..	OPEN
Oil cooler shutters (Mark III aircraft only)	..	Closed

(iii) Have each engine turned slowly by hand for at least two revolutions of the propeller, in order to ensure that oil will not cause a hydraulic lock of pistons or sleeves.

(iv) It is not necessary to prime the carburettors unless the aircraft has been standing for a week or more. If necessary, this must be done with the pressure balance cock (A) ON.

(v) High volatility fuel (Stores ref. 34A/111) should be used for priming at air temperatures below freezing. Instruct the ground crew to work the induction system priming pump until the suction and delivery pipes are primed. This may be judged by an increase in resistance.

(vi) Switch ON the ignition and press the starter and booster coil pushbuttons simultaneously for each engine in turn. Turning periods must not exceed 20 seconds, with a 30 seconds wait between each. The ground crew will prime the induction system of each engine while it is being turned, and the engine should start after the following number of strokes if cold:

Air temp. °C :	+30	+20	+10	0	−10	−20
A.M. Type B (small) pump						
Normal fuel		3	4	7	12	
High volatility fuel				4	8	18
Type K40 (large) pump						
Normal fuel		1	1	2	3	
High volatility fuel				1	2	5

(vii) Release the starter button as soon as the engine fires. It will probably be necessary to continue priming after the engine has fired and until it picks up on the carburettor.

(viii) As soon as the engine is running satisfactorily, release the booster coil button and get the ground crew to screw down the priming pump, turn OFF the priming cock and close the cowling door.

(ix) Open the engine up slowly to 1,000 r.p.m. and warm up at this speed.

---

41. Testing engines and installations

While warming up :

(i) Check temperatures and pressures, and test operation of the hydraulic system by lowering and raising the flaps.

(ii) Check the suction change-over cock and boost gauge reversal control.

(iii) Open up to 1,500 r.p.m. and test each magneto as a precautionary check.

After warming up to at least 15° C. oil temperature and 120° C. cylinder temperature, for each engine in turn:

(iv) At 1,500 r.p.m. change to high gear and observe the momentary drop in oil pressure which should return to normal within a few seconds. Change back to low gear.

(v) Open up to 2,400 r.p.m. and exercise and check operation of the constant speed propeller.

NOTE.—The following comprehensive checks should be carried out after repair, inspection other than daily, or otherwise at the pilot's discretion. Normally they may be reduced in accordance with local instructions.

(vi) Check supercharger high gear clutch engagement by setting the propeller control to give 2,400 r.p.m. (this may conveniently be done when exercising the propeller), then at 1,500 r.p.m. changing to high gear and opening up to maximum climbing boost. Observe that this boost is maintained without fluctuation for a few seconds. Change back to low gear.

(vii) (iv). With the propeller control fully forward open the throttle fully and check take-off boost and static r.p.m.

(viii) (v). Throttle back to maximum rich continuous boost and test each magneto in turn. The drop should not exceed 50 r.p.m.

42. Check list before taxying

Brake pressure	..	..	150 lb./sq.in (minm.).
Hatches	..	..	Closed
Fuel	..	..	Check contents
Pressure head heater		..	ON

43. Check list before take-off

T —Trimming tabs	..	All neutral
M—Mixture controls	..	NORMAL
P —Propeller controls	..	Levers fully forward
		Master switches ON
		Selector switches AUTO
F —Fuel pressure balance		
cock ..	.. ..	OFF (down)
Superchargers	..	MEDIUM
Carburettor air intakes		COLD
F —Flaps	.. ..	20° down
Auto-pilot	.. ..	Cock—OUT
		Clutch—IN
		Main switch—OFF
Gills ..	.. ..	One-third OPEN
Oil cooler shutters (Mk. III aircraft only)	..	Open as necessary
Throttle lever friction device	.. ..	Pulled back.

44. Take-off

(i) At 29,000 lb. get the tail well up and counteract any tendency to swing right by use of the rudder. If necessary, the starboard throttle should be opened slightly ahead of the port throttle.

(ii) At 33,000 lb. and over, the tendency to swing right is more pronounced and the aircraft should not be pulled off the ground at a speed lower than 85 m.p.h. (75 knots) I.A.S.

(iii) Increase speed to 125 m.p.h. (110 knots) I.A.S., which is the safety speed when taking off without flaps, then throttle back to climbing boost and reduce to climbing r.p.m. With 20° flap, safety speed is 115 m.p.h. (100 knots) I.A.S.

(iv) At a safe height of 6̶0̶0̶–̶8̶0̶0̶ feet raise the flaps.
400-500

45. Climbing

The speed for maximum rate of climb is initially 130 m.p.h. (115 knots) I.A.S.

46. General flying

(i) *Stability :* The aircraft is directionally and longitudinally stable, with only slight stability on the climb. Laterally, depressing a wing causes the nose to drop, with slow recovery of the wing.

(ii) *Controls:* When flying in bumpy weather, pilots may experience a slight "kick" on the controls, originating from the elevator and rudder. This does not interfere in any way with the control of the aircraft and can be ignored.

A.L.3
Part II
Para. 46
(iii) to
(vi)

(iii) *Change of trim :*

Undercarriage down	Nose slightly down
Flaps down	Nose up

The change of trim on lowering flaps is reduced by the permanent interconnection of the elevator trimming tabs with the flaps, but is not entirely eliminated. It is essential that the elevator trimming tab control *should not be forward of* the central position before the flaps are lowered, or damage to the tab control mechanism may result. On some aircraft a spring catch is fitted which allows the pilot to feel the central position on moving the control.

(iv) *Flying at low airspeeds :* At speeds below 125 m.p.h. (110 knots) I.A.S. it is more pleasant to fly with the flaps lowered 20°.

(v) *Supercharger exercising :* During a flight of several hours duration the supercharger gear should be changed at intervals of approximately two hours, and again prior to landing, in order to clear any sludge that may have accumulated in the clutch mechanism.

NOTE.—It is important not to change from low to high gear in flight below 5,000 feet unless the boost has been reduced to at least − 2 lb./sq.in., and at not more than 2,000 r.p.m.

A.L.4
Part II
Para. 46
(vi)

(vi) *Engine cutting with warm air :* On all aircraft on which Mods. N P.2036 and P.2204 are not incorporated, the operation of a hydraulic service with the carburettor air-intake control in t WARM position may cause engine cutting due to the shutt returning to the cold air position.

47. Stalling

(i) The stall with flaps and undercarriage down is normal. One wing usually drops fairly quickly, and as the aircraft heels over, the nose falls below the horizon.

(ii) *Stalling speeds in m.p.h. (knots) I.A.S. :*

	28,000 *lb.*	34,500 *lb.*
Flaps and undercarriage up..	70 (60)	78 (67)
Flaps and undercarriage down	58 (50)	64 (55)

48. Diving

A.L.1
Part II
Para. 48

(i) Leave the propeller speed controls at the cruising setting and (with electric propellers) the selector switches in the AUTO position.

(ii) Nose heaviness occurs at speeds in excess of approximately 280 m.p.h. (245 knots) I.A.S. and increases progressively with speed. When entering and during the early stages of the dive, therefore, the elevator trimmer must not be used to relieve the push force required on the control column. If, in emergency, the trimmer is used to assist recovery, care is necessary to avoid the pull-out becoming too rapid as speed falls off.

49. Check list before landing

Auto-pilot	Cock—OUT	
	Main switch—OFF	
Brake pressure	100 lb./sq.in. (minm.)	
Carburettor air intakes ..	COLD	
Gills	CLOSED	
Elevator trimming tabs ..	Neutral	
	(see para. 46(iii))	
Superchargers	MEDIUM	
Reduce speed to 140 m.p.h. (120 knots) I.A.S.		
U —Undercarriage	DOWN (check by lights and horn)	
M—Mixture controls	NORMAL	
P —Propeller controls ..	Levers fully forward	
	Selector switches— AUTO	

A.L.5
Part II
Para. 49

F —Fuel .. .. Nacelle tanks on
Flaps may be lowered to the take-off position at 140 m.p.h. (120 knots) I.A.S.
Reduce speed still further to 120 m.p.h. (105 knots) I.A.S.
F —Flaps .. .. Fully DOWN

NOTE.—Should failure of the interconnection (*see* Para. 15) be suspected (this will be indicated by the very large nose-up change of trim when the flaps are lowered), the flaps should be raised immediately and the landing made without them.

50. **Approach**

(i) Recommended approach speeds in m.p.h. (knots) I.A.S. are:

	26,000 *lb.*	29,000 *lb.*
Engine assisted	85 (75)	90 (80)
Glide	100 (85)	105 (90)
Flapless—engine assisted ..	105 (90)	110 (95)

(ii) If a flapless approach is necessary, trim well back and come in low with plenty of engine.

51. **Mislanding**

(i) The aircraft will climb with undercarriage and flaps down. At 28,000 lb. speed should be 90 m.p.h. (80 knots) I.A.S. until the flaps have been raised.

(ii) Raise the undercarriage immediately.

(iii) If the elevator tab control is aft of neutral it may be wound forward to central, but must not be forced past this position until the flaps have been raised.

(iv) Raise the flaps a little at a time at a safe height of about 500 feet.

- -

A.L.3
Part II
Para. 52

52. **After landing**

(i) Raise the flaps and open the cowling gills.

(ii) After taxying in, run the engines at 1,500 r.p.m. and change from low gear to high gear; after ten seconds change back to low gear.

(iii) Head the aircraft into wind and idle the engines at about 800 r.p.m. to cool them. Then open up gradually and evenly and run at −2 lb./sq.in. boost for five seconds; then throttle back slowly and evenly to 800 to 1,000 r.p.m. for two minutes before stopping.

NOTE.—If a backfire occurs after opening up to −2 lb./sq.in. boost, repeat the procedure.

(iv) Throttle back and stop the engines by pulling the slow-running cut-out controls.

(v) Switch OFF the ignition and turn OFF all fuel cocks.

(vi) Close the oil cooler shutters (Mark III aircraft only).

(vii) *Oil dilution* (*see* A.P. 2095):
The dilution period for these aircraft is 4 minutes and the operation should be carried out at an engine speed not exceeding 1,000 r.p.m.

53. **Beam approach**

(i) The recommended speeds (m.p.h. (knots) I.A.S.), r.p.m., boost (lb./sq.in.) and flap settings are:

	Maintaining height		Final approach
	Preliminary manœuvring	Manœuvring with u/c down	
Speed	130 (115)	130 (115)	100–105 (85–90)
Flaps	15°	15°	40° at O.M.B. Lower fully at I.M.B.
R.p.m.	2,000	2,400	Fully forward (AUTO)
Boost	—3	—1 to —2	—2 approx.

(ii) For change of trim see Para. 46(iii).

(iii) Approach at 600 feet over the O.M. Beacon, reducing to 100 feet over the I.M. Beacon.

NOTE.—Altimeter reads 50 feet at 100 feet.

(iv) Signal strength is best when flying parallel to the beam and weakest when flying away from it.

PART III

OPERATING DATA

54. Engine Data: Hercules XI (Mk. III aircraft only)

(i) *Fuel.*—100 octane.   (The reduced limitations for use with 87 octane fuel are shown in brackets.)

(ii) *Oil.*—See A.P.1464/C37.

(iii) *Engine limitations:*

		R.p.m.	Boost lb./sq.in.	Temp. °C. Cyl.	Oil inlet
MAX. TAKE-OFF TO 1,000 FT.	M	2,800	$+6\frac{3}{4}(+5)$	—	—
MAX. CLIMBING 1 HR. LIMIT	M S	2,500(2,400)	$+3\frac{1}{2}(+2\frac{1}{2})$	270	90
MAX. RICH .. CONTINUOUS	M S	2,500(2,400)	$+3\frac{1}{2}(+2\frac{1}{2})$	270 (250)	80
MAX. WEAK CONTINUOUS	M S	2,500(2,200)	zero	270 (250)	80
COMBAT .. 5 MINS. LIMIT	M S	2,800	$+6\frac{3}{4}(+5)$	280	100

OIL PRESSURE:

NORMAL ..	..	..	..	..	80 lb./sq.in.
MINIMUM	..	..	..	..	65 lb./sq.in.

MINM. OIL TEMP. FOR TAKE-OFF   ..   ..   5°C.

MAX. CYLR. TEMP. FOR STOPPING ENGINES   230°C.

55. Engine Data: Hercules VI, XVI and XVII

(i) *Fuel.*—100 octane. (The reduced limitations for use with 87 octane fuel are shown in brackets.)

(ii) *Oil.*—See A.P.1464/C37.

(iii) *Engine limitations :*

		R.p.m.	Boost lb./sq.in.	Temp. °C. Cyl.	Oil inlet
MAX. TAKE-OFF TO 1,000 FT.	M	2,800*	$+8\frac{1}{4}(+5)$	—	—
MAX. CLIMBING	M	2,400	$+6(+2\frac{1}{2})$	270	90
1 HR. LIMIT	S	2,500(2,400)	$+6(+2\frac{1}{2})$	270	90
MAX. RICH CONTINUOUS..	M S	2,400	$+6(+2\frac{1}{2})$	270(250)	80
MAX. WEAK CONTINUOUS ..	M S	2,400, (2,200	$+2$†(zero)	270(25c)	80
COMBAT 5 MINS. LIMIT..	M S	2,800	$+8\frac{1}{4}(+5)$	280	100

* 2,900 on Hercules XVII engines.
† Weak mixture on Hercules XVI and XVII engines is obtained by keeping at or below $+2$ lb./sq.in. boost.

OIL PRESSURE:
NORMAL	80 lb./sq.in.
MINIMUM	65 lb./sq.in.

MINM. OIL TEMP. FOR TAKE-OFF.. .. 5°C.
MAX. CYLR. TEMP. FOR STOPPING ENGINES 230°C.

56. Flying limitations

(i) These aircraft are designed for manœuvres appropriate to a medium bomber and care must be taken to avoid imposing excessive loads in recovery from dives and in turns at high speeds.
Spinning and aerobatics are not permitted.

(ii) *Maximum speeds in m.p.h. (knots) I.A.S.*
Diving (A.U.W. *below* 34,500 lb.)	320 (280)
Diving (A.U.W. *above* 34,500 lb.)	280 (245)
Leigh light lowered	230 (200)
Undercarriage DOWN	140 (120)
Flaps down to take-off position	140 (120)
Flaps fully DOWN	120 (105)
Landing lamps lowered	100 (85)

II
56

(iii) *Maximum weights:*

   (a) *Mark III aircraft:*

   Take-off and straight flying   ..   ..   34,500 lb.
   All forms of flying and landing   ..   ..   29,000 lb.

   (b) *Mark X, XI, XII, XIII and XIV aircraft:*

   Take-off and straight flying   ..   ..   36,500 lb.
   All forms of flying and landing   ..   ..   30,500 lb.

   NOTE.—On Mark X, XI and XII aircraft on which
   Modification No. P.1603 has not been embodied
   the maximum A.U.W. is 34,500 lb.

   The maximum landing weight for all Marks when
   used for training purposes is 29,000 lb.

(iv) *Bomb clearance angles :*

   Diving   ..   ..   60°
   Climbing   ..   ..   20°

57. Position error corrections

From To ..	100 130	130 140	140 150	150 170	170 190	190 200	200 220	220 240	240 270	}m.p.h. ∫I.A.S.
Add .. Subtract	12 —	10 —	8 —	6 —	4 —	2 —	0 0	— 2	— 4	m.p.h. m.p.h.
From .. To ..	85 110	110 120	120 130	130 145	145 165	165 170	170 190	190 205	205 230	}knots ∫I.A.S.
Add .. Subtract	12 —	10 —	8 —	6 —	4 —	2 —	0 0	— 2	— 4	knots knots

NOTE.—When the A.S.I. is connected to the static vent
   the above corrections to airspeed can be ignored.

58. Maximum performance

Mark III and X aircraft:

 (i) *Climbing :* 130 m.p.h. (115 knots) I.A.S.

   Change to S ratio when the boost has fallen by 3 lb./sq.in.
   (Mk. X aircraft: $2\frac{1}{2}$ lb/sq.in.)

 (ii) *Combat :* Use S ratio if the boost in M ratio is 3 lb./sq.in.
   below the maximum permitted.

59. **Economical flying** (*see* curves Page 32)

(i) *Climbing:*

Fly at 130 m.p.h. (115 knots) I.A.S. in rich mixture at maximum climbing boost and r.p.m. Change to S ratio when boost has fallen by 3 lb./sq.in. (Mark III and X aircraft only.)

To improve fuel consumption, if temperatures are not excessive, the boost should be followed back with the throttle as far as the economical cruising boost position (Hercules VI or XI), or to the midway position (Hercules XVI or XVII). A weak mixture climb at full load is not recommended, but when used change to S ratio when boost has fallen by 2 lb./sq.in.

(ii) *Cruising:*

(*a*) The recommended speeds m.p.h. (knots) I.A.S. are as follows:

Medium and high altitudes:

Fully loaded (outward journey)	..	..	155 (135)
Lightly loaded (homeward journey)		..	140 (125)

Low altitudes:

For maximum range	..	..	..	160 (140)
For maximum endurance	..		..	145–150 (125–130)

(*b*) Fly in weak mixture and M ratio at the maximum permissible boost (on some aircraft this position of the throttle lever is indicated by a white line on the lever coinciding with a pointer on the quadrant, pending the introduction of a warning light) and reduce speed by reducing r.p.m., which may be as low as 1,650 if this will give the recommended speed. If at 1,650 r.p.m. the recommended speed is exceeded, reduce boost.

(*c*) Engage S ratio when the recommended speed cannot be maintained at 2,400 r.p.m. (2,500 r.p.m. on Mark III aircraft if using 100 octane fuel), but not below 15,000 feet.

(iii) On Mark III aircraft the use of warm air intakes will not appreciably affect air miles per gallon, but on the later Marks they will be reduced by about $5\frac{1}{2}\%$.

(iv) The effect of small gill openings when cruising is insignificant.

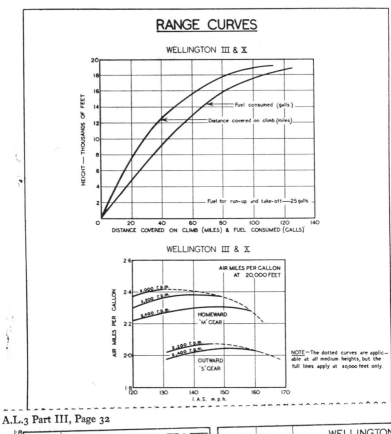

RANGE CURVES

WELLINGTON III & X

Fuel consumed (galls.)

Distance covered on climb (miles)

Fuel for run-up and take-off—25 galls.

HEIGHT — THOUSANDS OF FEET

DISTANCE COVERED ON CLIMB (MILES) & FUEL CONSUMED (GALLS)

WELLINGTON III & X

AIR MILES PER GALLON AT 20,000 FEET

2,000 r.p.m.

2,200 r.p.m.

2,400 r.p.m.

HOMEWARD 'M' GEAR

2,200 r.p.m.

2,400 r.p.m.

OUTWARD 'S' GEAR

AIR MILES PER GALLON

I.A.S. m.p.h.

NOTE—The dotted curves are applicable at all medium heights, but the full lines apply at 20,000 feet only.

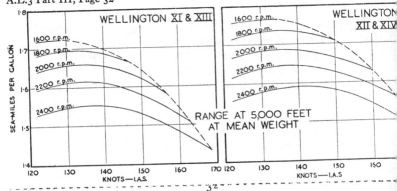

WELLINGTON XI & XIII

1600 r.p.m.
1800 r.p.m.
2000 r.p.m.
2200 r.p.m.
2400 r.p.m.

WELLINGTON XII & XIV

1600 r.p.m.
1800 r.p.m.
2000 r.p.m.
2200 r.p.m.
2400 r.p.m.

SEA-MILES PER GALLON

RANGE AT 5,000 FEET AT MEAN WEIGHT

KNOTS—I.A.S

KNOTS—I.A.S

60. Fuel capacities and consumption

(i) *Capacities*

(*a*) *Normal:*

Two front wing tanks	300 gallons
Two rear wing tanks	334 gallons
Two nacelle tanks	116 gallons
Total	750 gallons

(*b*) *Long-range (totals):*

With *one* 140–gallon tank	890 gallons
With *one* 185-gallon tank	935 gallons
With *one* 140-gallon tank and *two* 55-gallon tanks	1,000 gallons
With *two* 140-gallon tanks	1,030 gallons
With *one* 295-gallon tank	1,045 gallons
With *one* 185-gallon tank and *one* 140-gallon tank	1,075 gallons
With *three* 185-gallon tanks	1,305 gallons

(ii) *Hercules XI (Mark III aircraft only) fuel consumptions:*

(*a*) The approximate total consumptions in RICH mixture are as follows:

Boost lb./sq.in	R.p.m.	Galls./hr.
+6¾	2,800	290
+3½	2,500	222

(*b*) The approximate total consumptions (galls./hr.) in WEAK mixture are as follows:

Boost lb./sq.in.	M ratio at 10,000 ft.			S ratio at 15,000 ft.		
	R.p.m.			R.p.m.		
	2,400	2,200	2,000	2,400	2,200	2,000
0	117	—	—	111	104	—
−1	111	102	—	107	98	92
−2	104	96	85	101	92	87
−3	96	88	79	96	87	81
−4	87	81	73	90	81	75

For every 2,000 ft. *above* these heights *add* 1 gall./hr.
For every 2,000 ft. *below* these heights *deduct* 1 gall./hr.

(iii) *Hercules VI, XVI and XVII fuel consumptions:*

(*a*) The approximate total consumptions in RICH mixture are as follows:

Boost lb./sq.in.	*R.p.m.*	*Galls./hr.*
+8	2,900	320
+6	2,400	239

(*b*) The approximate total consumptions (galls./hr.) in WEAK mixture are as follows:

Boost lb./sq.in.	M ratio at 5,000 ft.*				S ratio at 15,000 ft.			
	R.p.m.				R.p.m.			
	2,400	2,200	2,000	1,800	2,400	2,200	2,000	1,800
+2	118	110	102	94	116	110	106	96
0	106	98	92	80	104	100	96	88ᶠ
−2	94	88	82	74	94	90	86	80ᶜ
−4	84	80	74	68	86	82	78	—

For every 1,000 ft. *above* heights quoted *add* ½ gall /hr.

For every 1,000 ft. *below* heights quoted *deduct* ½ gall./hr.

* For Hercules XVII engines these figures should be increased by five.

61. **Static vent speeds**

The following table shows the various handling speeds in m.p.h. and equivalent knots for aircraft with the A.S.I. connected to the static vent:

	M.p.h.	*Knots*
Take-off speed (minimum)	95	85
Safety speed—no flaps	135	120
Safety speed—20° flap	125	110
Climbing speed (initial)	140	125
Flying at low airspeeds (20° flap) ..	135	120

Stalling speeds:

At 28,500 lb.—all up	85–90	75–80
At 28,500 lb.—all down	70–80	60–70
At 34,500 lb.—all up	95–100	85–90
At 34,500 lb.—all down	80–90	70–80

Circuit speeds:

Before lowering flaps	..	..	150	130
After lowering flaps..	..	..	130	115

Approach speeds:

At 26,000 lb.—engine assisted	..		95	85
At 26,000 lb.—glide	..	..	110	95
At 26,000 lb.—flapless—engine assisted	..	..	..	115	100
At 29,000 lb.—engine assisted	..	100	90
At 29,000 lb.—glide	..	115	100
At 29,000 lb.—flapless—engine assisted	..	..	..	120	105

Mislanding	..	..	..	..	100	90
Beam approach—initial	..	..	140	125
Beam approach—final	..	..	110–115	95–100

Maximum speeds:

Diving	..	..	..	..	310	270
Leigh light lowered ..	..	..	230	200
Undercarriage down	..	..	150	130
Flaps down to T.O. position	..	150	130
Flaps fully down	..	..	..	130	115
Landing lamp lowered	..	..	110	95

Economical flying:

Climbing	..	..	..	..	140	125

Cruising (Medium and high altitudes)

Fully loaded	..	..	..	160	140
Lightly loaded ..	..	..	150	130

Cruising (Low altitudes)

Max. range	..	..	..	165	145
Max. endurance	..	..	150–155	130–135

Engine failure during take-off	..	125	110
Single engine flight	..	..	..	$\left\{\begin{array}{l}135 \\ 130\end{array}\right.$	120 115

Fuel jettisoning:

Flaps up	..	..	..	..	110	95
Flaps down 20°	..	..	..	135	120
Flaps fully down	..	..	..	90	80

PART IV

EMERGENCIES

62. **Engine failure during take-off**

(i) With flaps 20° down the aircraft can be held straight if 115 m.p.h. (100 knots) I.A.S. has been attained.

(ii) Any bombs, depth-charges, or torpedoes should be jettisoned. The propeller of the dead engine should be feathered and the gills closed.

(iii) With the starboard engine failed it should be possible to climb away at about 31,000 lb. With the port engine failed performance is slightly inferior.

63. **Engine failure in flight**

(i) Turn ON the fuel pressure balance cock (A). If the dead engine does not pick up, showing that the fuel pump is not the cause of failure, turn OFF the cock. If it is desired to run the live engine on the tanks in the opposite wing, it is necessary for the crew to open the suction balance cock (B).

(ii) The propeller of the dead engine must be feathered and the gills closed.

(iii) Fly in M ratio at 2,500 r.p.m. and $+3\frac{1}{2}$ lb./sq.in. boost (Mark III aircraft), or 2,400 r.p.m. and $+6$ lb./sq.in. boost (later Marks), at 125 m.p.h. (110 knots) I.A.S. (If using 87 octane fuel the r.p.m. and boost are 2,400 and $2\frac{1}{2}$ lb./sq.in. respectively for all Marks of aircraft.) If necessary to maintain height, speed may be reduced to 120 m.p.h. (105 knots) I.A.S. Cylinder temperatures of the live engine must be watched and the gills opened as necessary. They should not be opened excessively as performance deteriorates. If temperatures do rise too high, increase speed.

Climbing boost and r.p.m. should not be exceeded except to prevent dangerous loss of height. In tropical conditions 125 m.p.h. (110 knots) I.A.S. is the speed for minimum rate of descent.

(iv) To maintain height at climbing power when using 100 octane fuel, weight must be reduced to approximately 28,500 lb. by jettisoning all bombs, depth-charges, or torpedoes, and, if necessary, some of the fuel load (*see* Para. 68). At 120 m.p.h. (105 knots) I.A.S., it should be possible to maintain height at 2,000 feet at this weight in temperate conditions. With full rudder trim a small amount of bank is required at this speed to reduce foot load.

64. **Feathering**

(i) *Rotol electric propellers:*

(*a*) Close the throttle immediately.

(*b*) Set the feathering switch to FEATHER, or pull out and depress the knob of the selector switch (see Para. 23(ii)(*c*)), (if time is available use DEC. R.P.M.).

(*c*) Turn off the fuel supply to the engine which is to be stopped.

(*d*) Set the selector switch central (only if the feathering switch is separate).

(*e*) Switch off the ignition when the engine has stopped or nearly stopped.

(ii) *Rotol hydraulic propellers:*

(*a*) Close the throttle immediately.

(*b*) Set the propeller speed control fully back through the gate and turn off the fuel supply to the engine which is to be stopped.

(*c*) Hold the button in until feathering is completed.

(*d*) Switch off the ignition when the engine has stopped or nearly stopped.

(iii) *D. H. Hydromatic propellers:*

(*a*) Close the throttle immediately.

(*b*) Hold the button in only long enough to ensure that it stays in by itself; then release it so that it can spring out when feathering is completed.

(*c*) Turn off the fuel supply to the engine which is to be stopped.

(*d*) Switch off the ignition when the engine has stopped or nearly stopped.

65. Unfeathering

(i) *Rotol electric propellers:*

(*a*) Set the throttle closed or slightly open, the propeller speed control fully down and switch on ignition.

(*b*) Set the feathering switch to NORMAL and hold the selector switch to INC. R.P.M. until about 1,000 r.p.m. are reached. Then set the selector switch to AUTO.

(ii) *Rotol hydraulic propellers:*

(*a*) Set the throttle closed or slightly open and switch on ignition.

(*b*) Set the propeller speed control just forward of the gate.

(*c*) Hold the button in until normal constant-speed operation is resumed. If unfeathering does not start when the button is depressed, set the propeller speed control slightly forward (to take up backlash).

A.L.4
Part IV
Para. 65
(iii)

(iii) *D.H. Hydromatic propellers:*

(*a*) Set the throttle closed or slightly open, the propeller speed control fully back and switch on ignition.

(*b*) Hold the button in until r.p.m. reach 800 to 1,000.

(*c*) If the propeller does not return to normal constant-speed operation, refeather and then unfeather again at a slightly higher r.p.m.

A.L.3
Part IV
Para. 66

66. Undercarriage emergency operation

If the undercarriage cannot be lowered in the normal way by the engine-driven pump, a reserve supply of fluid and separate pipe lines can be brought into use by operating the emergency hydraulic selector (82) and the handpump (81).

Modified Mark III and X aircraft are fitted with a compressed air system operated by a white T handle above the undercarriage and flap selector levers. The undercarriage cannot be raised after the compressed air has been used. On some of these aircraft the emergency hydraulic system may be used for operating the other services, depending on the scheme fitted. The recommended method of operation is as follows (in all cases the normal selector must first be operated):

(i) *Unmodified aircraft:*

(*a*) Move the emergency hydraulic selector to EMERGENCY and operate the handpump (at least 250 strokes will be required).
(*b*) Return the selector to NORMAL and attempt to lower the flaps by the normal method.

(ii) *Modified Mk. III and X aircraft :*

Scheme A

(a) Lower the undercarriage by air pressure.

(b) Attempt to lower the flaps by the normal method.

Scheme B

(a) Lower the undercarriage by air pressure.

(b) If this fails, try the emergency handpump method.

(c) Return the emergency selector to NORMAL and attempt to lower the flaps by the normal method.

Scheme C

(a) Lower the undercarriage by air pressure.

(b) With the emergency selector at EMERGENCY the hand-pump may be used for lowering the flaps.

Scheme D

(a) Lower the undercarriage by air pressure.

(b) With the emergency selector at EMERGENCY the hand-pump may be used to operate any service selected by the normal selectors.

Scheme E

As scheme D, except that the bomb doors cannot be operated with the emergency selector at EMERGENCY.

67. Bomb and Depth-charge jettisoning

(i) Open the bomb doors.

(ii) Jettison any small bomb containers first by operating the switch (75) on the starboard side of the cockpit.

(iii) Jettison the bombs or depth-charges by pulling the handle (2) on the port side of the instrument panel.

(iv) Close the bomb doors.

68. Fuel jettisoning

(i) Fuel in the four main tanks only may be jettisoned by first unscrewing the air vent valve wheel (51) on the left of the instrument panel four turns and then rotating the jettison valve wheel (52) immediately above to open. On later aircraft the two valves are operated by a single control. After jettisoning, the valves must be closed to maintain buoyancy or prevent fire. They can be closed if necessary when only part of the fuel has been jettisoned.

(ii) The average rates of jettisoning are as follows:

(*a*) Flaps up at 100 m.p.h. (85 knots) I.A.S.: 100 gallons in 25 seconds.

(*b*) Flaps lowered 20° at 125 m.p.h. (110 knots) I.A.S.: 100 gallons in 20 seconds.

(*c*) Flaps fully down at 80 m.p.h. (70 knots) I.A.S.: 100 gallons in 15 seconds.

69. **Parachute exits**

When abandoning the aircraft by parachute the main entrance hatch and the starboard push-out panel immediately aft of the beam guns should be used as exits. A foot lever at the starboard side of the main entrance hatch enables the door to be opened independently of the door release handle. To gain access to the starboard push-out panel, a wooden guard or cover, fixed to the frame by press-studs, must be pulled away. The cover is inscribed PULL OFF COVER FOR ACCESS TO EMERGENCY EXIT.

70. **Crash exits**

In addition to the foregoing exits, roof exits are provided in the pilot's cockpit and at the sextant station. In the former, two outwardly-opening doors in the cockpit roof are released by a central lever and in the latter the sextant dome is released for opening downwards by either of two spring-loaded bolt levers at the front and rear of the mounting. These exits, together with the other unobstructed exits, can be used by the crew in the event of a crash-landing.

71. **Air/sea rescue equipment**

(i) A " J " type dinghy is stowed in the starboard engine nacelle and is secured by a painter of 150 lbs. breaking strength. It may be inflated and released by any of the following methods:

(*a*) Manually by pulling the handle inside the fuselage at the top of the rear face of the main spar, on the extreme starboard side. A sustained direct pull towards the centre of the aircraft is necessary.

(*b*) By ripping the fabric patch on the top surface of the starboard wing, about 2 feet from the fuselage side, immediately behind the main spar. This exposes a handle which is retained in spring clips immediately below the patch. A sustained pull upwards and inboard is necessary.

(*c*) Automatically by flooding of the immersion switch in the starboard engine nacelle.

(ii) Certain aircraft have a small stowage for the dinghy permitting only the following items to be stowed with the dinghy: topping-up bellows, leak stoppers and drogue. On these aircraft the remaining air-sea rescue equipment is carried in a Type 5 and a Type 7 emergency packs (Stores References 27.C./1919 and /1931 respectively), these being stowed in the fuselage against the front spar. Their contents are given in the current Appendix A for the aircraft.

(iii) On most aircraft, however, the dinghy compartment is larger, having the rear portion of the stowage floor stepped down, and a special emergency pack is carried in the stepped-down portion of the stowage and secured to the dinghy life-line by a lanyard. In addition, a Type 7 emergency pack is stowed inside the fuselage, aft of the front spar.

72. Flotation gear

Fourteen inflatable flotation bags are stowed at the top of the bomb cells. These bags are inflated from three CO_2 cylinders stowed in the port and starboard inner planes, which are discharged separately by pulling each of three handles contained in a box attached to the rear of the spar centre section and covered by an inscribed tear-off patch.

An immersion switch, mounted immediately aft of the front turret, automatically inflates the flotation bags when immersed in salt water, but in view of the time lag and the fact that the bomb doors may collapse upon impact unless supported, the bags should be inflated by means of the manual controls while still in the air. Before inflating the flotation bags, the bomb doors must be opened and bombs, or depth charges, jettisoned and the doors then closed again.

NOTE.—Flotation gear is not fitted when torpedoes are carried.

73. Ditching

(i) Bombs, depth-charges, or torpedoes should be jettisoned and the bomb doors then closed.

(ii) The mid-under turret on Mk. XII and XIV aircraft should be retracted.

(iii) The flotation bags should, if possible, be inflated at least five minutes before ditching, but not above 3,000 feet in altitude. A member of the crew should check by examination through the windows at the rear end of the bomb cell that the bags have been properly inflated and advise the captain accordingly.

(iv) Flaps should be lowered 30°.

74. Turret external rotation

To gain access to them in an emergency, the front (if fitted) and rear gun turrets can be rotated to the central position by means of nearby external rotation valves in the hydraulic supply lines on the port and starboard sides of the fuselage respectively.

Each valve is brought into operation by forcing a wire-locked oil supply change-over lever into the ON position; the turret can then be rotated in either direction by operating the lever on the other end of the valve unit.

A.L.4
Part IV
Para. 75

75. Fire-extinguishers

Each engine nacelle is fitted with a Graviner type fire-extinguishing system operated by a corresponding pushbutton (19) on the right-hand side of the instrument panel. Automatic operation is by impact and gravity switches inside the fuselage. On later aircraft flame switches operate two red warning lights above the pushbuttons or on the centre of the instrument panel. One or more portable extinguishers are stowed at convenient points within the fuselage.

PART V

ILLUSTRATIONS

KEY TO *Fig. 1*

1. Bomb steering indicator.
2. Bomb/depth charge jettison control.
3. Auto-controls pressure gauge.
4. Instrument flying panel.
5. Starter and booster coil pushbuttons—port engine.
6. Propeller feathering switch—port engine.
7. Port engine speed indicator.
8. Undercarriage warning horn test pushbutton.
9. Fuel contents gauges pushbutton.
10. Windscreen wiper controls.
11. Undercarriage indicator.
12. Boost gauges (two).
13. Starboard engine speed indicator.
14. Cylinder temperature gauges (two).
15. Propeller feathering switch—starboard engine.
16. Oil tank low-level warning lights (two).
17. Starter and booster coil pushbuttons—starboard engine.
18. Pneumatic pressure gauge.
19. Fire extinguisher pushbuttons (two).
20. Air temperature gauge.
21. D.F. indicator.
22. Fuel pressure warning lights (two).
23. Pilot's call light.
24. Flare launching warning light.
25. Suction gauge.
26. Oil pressure gauges (two).
27. Oil temperature gauge—starboard engine.
28. Boost gauge reversal control.
29. Flap control lever.
30. Compass.
31. Undercarriage selector lever.
32. Rudder pedal—starboard.
33. Windscreen de-icing pump
34. Oil temperature gauge—port engine.
35. Rudder bar adjustment wheel.
36. Flap indicator.
37. Cowling gill controls (two).
38. Intercomm. microphone pushbutton.
39. Torpedo release pushbuttons (two).
40. Brake lever.
41. Brake locking slide.
42. Bomb release pushbutton.
43. Bomb doors control.
44. Landing lamps switch.
45. Bomb master switch.